OUT
OF
DANGER

Terminal Moraine (1972)

Children in Exile: Poems 1968–1984 (1984)

You Were Marvellous (1983)

Partingtime Hall (with John Fuller, 1987)

All the Wrong Places: Adrift in the Politics of the Pacific Rim (1988)

Out of Danger (1994)

OUT
OF
DANGER

[JAMES FENTON]

FARRAR STRAUS GIROUX

NEW YORK

Copyright © 1994 by James Fenton
All rights reserved
Printed in the United States of America
Published simultaneously in Canada by HarperCollins*CanadaLtd*
Published in the United Kingdom by Penguin Books, Ltd
First American edition, 1994
Second printing, 1994
LIBRARY OF CONGRESS CATALOGING-IN-PUBLICATION DATA
Fenton, James.
Out of danger / James Fenton.—1st American ed.
p.   cm.
I. Title.
PR6056.E53093   1994   93-40178
821'.914—dc20   CIP

To D. E. P.

Contents

I

Out of Danger

Beauty, Danger and Dismay   3
Out of Danger   4
Serious   5
The Ideal   6
Hinterhof   7
The Possibility   8
The Mistake   9
I'll Explain   11
In Paris with You   12
The Milkfish Gatherers   14
Jerusalem   18
For Andrew Wood   22

II

Out of the East

Out of the East   27
Blood and Lead   34
The Ballad of the Imam and the Shah   35
I Saw a Child   39
Tiananmen   41
The Ballad of the Shrieking Man   43
Fireflies of the Sea   48
Cut-Throat Christ   50

Gabriel 55
The Ballad of the Birds 57
I Know What I'm Missing 61
Bruisers and Dreamers 63
Here Come the Drum Majorettes! 65

III

Maski Paps

The Orange Dove of Fiji 71
The Journey 73
On a Recent Indiscretion by a Certain Fulbright Fellow in
    Upper Egypt 75
Maski Papaano 77

IV

The Manila Manifesto 81

Notes 104

I

Out of Danger

Beauty, Danger and Dismay

Beauty, danger and dismay
Met me on the public way.
Whichever I chose, I chose dismay.

Out of Danger

Heart be kind and sign the release
As the trees their loss approve.
Learn as leaves must learn to fall
Out of danger, out of love.

What belongs to frost and thaw
Sullen winter will not harm.
What belongs to wind and rain
Is out of danger from the storm.

Jealous passion, cruel need
Betray the heart they feed upon.
But what belongs to earth and death
Is out of danger from the sun.

I was cruel, I was wrong –
Hard to say and hard to know.
You do not belong to me.
You are out of danger now –

Out of danger from the wind,
Out of danger from the wave,
Out of danger from the heart
Falling, falling out of love.

Serious

Awake, alert,
Suddenly serious in love,
You're a surprise.
I've known you long enough –
Now I can hardly meet your eyes.

It's not that I'm
Embarrassed or ashamed.
You've changed the rules
The way I'd hoped they'd change
Before I thought: hopes are for fools.

Let me walk with you.
I've got the newspapers to fetch.
I think you know
I think you have the edge
But I feel cheerful even so.

That's why I laughed.
That's why I went and kicked that stone.
I'm serious!
That's why I cartwheeled home.
This should mean something. Yes, it does.

The Ideal

This is where I came from.
I passed this way.
This should not be shameful
Or hard to say.

A self is a self.
It is not a screen.
A person should respect
What he has been.

This is my past
Which I shall not discard.
This is the ideal.
This is hard.

Hinterhof

Stay near to me and I'll stay near to you —
As near as you are dear to me will do,
    Near as the rainbow to the rain,
    The west wind to the windowpane,
As fire to the hearth, as dawn to dew.

Stay true to me and I'll stay true to you —
As true as you are new to me will do,
    New as the rainbow in the spray,
    Utterly new in every way,
New in the way that what you say is true.

Stay near to me, stay true to me. I'll stay
As near, as true to you as heart could pray.
    Heart never hoped that one might be
    Half of the things you are to me —
The dawn, the fire, the rainbow and the day.

The Possibility

The lizard on the wall, engrossed,
The sudden silence from the wood
Are telling me that I have lost
The possibility of good.

I know this flower is beautiful
And yesterday it seemed to be.
It opened like a crimson hand.
It was not beautiful to me.

I know that work is beautiful.
It is a boon. It is a good.
Unless my working were a way
Of squandering my solitude.

And solitude was beautiful
When I was sure that I was strong.
I thought it was a medium
In which to grow, but I was wrong.

The jays are swearing in the wood.
The lizard moves with ugly speed.
The flower closes like a fist.
The possibility recedes.

The Mistake

With the mistake your life goes in reverse.
Now you can see exactly what you did
Wrong yesterday and wrong the day before
And each mistake leads back to something worse

And every nuance of your hypocrisy
Towards yourself, and every excuse
Stands solidly on the perspective lines
And there is perfect visibility.

What an enlightenment. The colonnade
Rolls past on either side. You needn't move.
The statues of your errors brush your sleeve.
You watch the tale turn back – and you're dismayed.

And this dismay at this, this big mistake
Is made worse by the sight of all those who
Knew all along where these mistakes would lead –
Those frozen friends who watched the crisis break.

Why didn't they *say*? Oh, but they did indeed –
Said with a murmur when the time was wrong
Or by a mild refusal to assent
Or told you plainly but you would not heed.

Yes, you can hear them now. It hurts. It's worse
Than any sneer from any enemy.
Take this dismay. Lay claim to this mistake.
Look straight along the lines of this reverse.

I'll Explain

It's something you say at your peril.
It's something you shouldn't contain.
It's a truth for the dark and a pillow.
Turn out the light and I'll explain.

It's the obvious truth of the morning
Bitten back as the sun turns to rain,
To the rain, to the dark, to the pillow.
Turn out the light and I'll explain.

> It's what I was hoping to tell you.
> It's what I was hoping you'd guess.
> It's what I was hoping you *wouldn't* guess
> Or you wouldn't mind.
> It's a kind
> Of hopelessness.

It's the hope that you hope at your peril.
It's the hope that you fear to attain.
It's the obvious truth of the evening.
Turn out the light and I'll explain.

In Paris with You

Don't talk to me of love. I've had an earful
And I get tearful when I've downed a drink or two.
I'm one of your talking wounded.
I'm a hostage. I'm maroonded.
But I'm in Paris with you.

Yes I'm angry at the way I've been bamboozled
And resentful at the mess that I've been through.
I admit I'm on the rebound
And I don't care where are *we* bound.
I'm in Paris with you.

> Do you mind if we do *not* go to the Louvre,
> If we say sod off to sodding Notre Dame,
> If we skip the Champs Elysées
> And remain here in this sleazy
> Old hotel room
> Doing this and that
> To what and whom
> Learning who you are,
> Learning what I am.

Don't talk to me of love. Let's talk of Paris,
The little bit of Paris in our view.
There's that crack across the ceiling
And the hotel walls are peeling
And I'm in Paris with you.

Don't talk to me of love. Let's talk of Paris.
I'm in Paris with the slightest thing you do.
I'm in Paris with your eyes, your mouth,
I'm in Paris with . . . all points south.
Am I embarrassing you?
I'm in Paris with you.

The Milkfish Gatherers

TO G.L.

The sea sounds insincere
Giving and taking with one hand.
It stopped a river here last month
Filling its mouth with sand.

They drag the shallows for the milkfish fry —
Two eyes on a glass noodle, nothing more.
Roused by his vigilant young wife
The drowsy stevedore

Comes running barefoot past the swamp
To meet a load of wood.
The yellow peaked cap, the patched pink shorts
Seem to be all his worldly goods.

The nipa booths along the coast
Protect the milkfish gatherers' rights.
Nothing goes unobserved. My good custodian
Sprawls in the deckchair through the night.

Take care, he says, take care —
Not everybody is a friend.
And so he makes my life more private still —
A privacy on which he will attend.

But the dogs are sly with the garbage
And the cats ruthless, even with sliced bread,

As the terns are ruthless among the shoals.
Men watch the terns, then give the boat its head

Dragging a wide arc through the blue,
Trailing their lines,
Cutting the engine out
At the first sign.

A hundred feet away
Something of value struggles not to die.
It will sell for a dollar a kilo.
It weighs two kilos on the line – a prize.

And the hull fills with a fortune
And the improbable colours of the sea
But the spine lives when the brain dies
In a convulsive misery.

Rummagers of inlets, scourers of the deep,
Dynamite men, their bottles crammed with wicks,
They named the sea's inhabitants with style –
The slapped vagina fish, the horse's dick.

Polillo 'melts' means it is far away –
The smoking island plumed from slash and burn.
And from its shore, busy with hermit crabs,
Look to Luzon. Infanta melts in turn.

The setting sun behind the Sierra Madre
Projects a sharp blue line across the sky
And in the eastern glow beyond Polillo
It looks as if another sun might rise –

As if there were no night,
Only a brother evening and a dawn.
No night! No death! How could these people live?
How could the pressure lanterns lure the prawns?

Nothing of value has arrived all day —
No timber, no rattan. Now after dark,
The news comes from the sea. They crowd the beach
And prime a lantern, waiting for the shark.

The young receive the gills, which they will cook.
The massive liver wallows on the shore
And the shark's teeth look like a row of sharks
Advancing along a jaw.

Alone again by spirit light
I notice something happening on a post.
Something has burst its skin and now it hangs,
Hangs for dear life onto its fine brown ghost.

Clinging exhausted to its former self,
Its head flung back as if to watch the moon,
The blue-green veins pulsing along its wings,
The thing unwraps itself, but falls too soon.

The ants are tiny and their work is swift —
The insect-shark is washed up on their land —
While the sea sounds insincere,
Giving and taking with one hand.

At dawn along the seashore come
The milkfish gatherers, human fry.
A white polythene bowl
Is what you need to sort the milkfish by.

For a hatched fish is a pair of eyes –
There is nothing more to see.
But the spine lives when the brain dies
In a convulsive misery.

Jerusalem

I

Stone cries to stone,
  Heart to heart, heart to stone,
And the interrogation will not die
  For there is no eternal city
  And there is no pity
And there is nothing underneath the sky
  No rainbow and no guarantee –
There is no covenant between your God and me.

II

It is superb in the air.
  Suffering is everywhere
And each man wears his suffering like a skin.
  My history is proud.
  Mine is not allowed.
This is the cistern where all wars begin,
  The laughter from the armoured car.
This is the man who won't believe you're what you are.

III

This is your fault.
  This is a crusader vault.
The Brook of Kidron flows from Mea She'arim.
  I will pray for you.
  I will tell you what to do.

I'll stone you. I shall break your every limb.
  Oh I am not afraid of you
But maybe I should fear the things you make me do.

  IV

  This is not Golgotha.
  This is the Holy Sepulchre,
The Emperor Hadrian's temple to a love
  Which he did not much share.
  Golgotha could be anywhere.
Jerusalem itself is on the move.
  It leaps and leaps from hill to hill
And as it makes its way it also makes its will.

  V

  The city was sacked.
  Jordan was driven back.
The pious Christians burned the Jews alive.
  This is a minaret.
  I'm not finished yet.
We're waiting for reinforcements to arrive.
  What was your mother's real name?
Would it be safe today to go to Bethlehem?

  VI

  This is the Garden Tomb.
  No, *this* is the Garden Tomb.
I'm an Armenian. I am a Copt.
  This is Utopia.
  I came here from Ethiopia.
This hole is where the flying carpet dropped
  The Prophet off to pray one night
And from here one hour later he resumed his flight.

VII

    Who packed your bag?

    I packed my bag.

  Where was your uncle's mother's sister born?

    Have you ever met an Arab?

    Yes I am a scarab.

  I am a worm. I am a thing of scorn.

    I cry Impure from street to street

And see my degradation in the eyes I meet.

VIII

    I am your enemy.

    This is Gethsemane.

  The broken graves look to the Temple Mount.

    Tell me now, tell me when

    When shall we all rise again?

  Shall I be first in that great body count?

    When shall the tribes be gathered in?

When, tell me, when shall the Last Things begin?

IX

    You are in error.

    This is terror.

  This is your banishment. This land is mine.

    This is what you earn.

    This is the Law of No Return.

  This is the sour dough, this the sweet wine.

    This is my history, this my race

And this unhappy man threw acid in my face.

X

Stone cries to stone,

Heart to heart, heart to stone.

These are the warrior archaeologists.

This is us and that is them.

This is Jerusalem.

These are the dying men with tattooed wrists.

Do this and I'll destroy your home.

I have destroyed your home. You have destroyed my home.

December 1988

For Andrew Wood

What would the dead want from us
Watching from their cave?
Would they have us forever howling?
Would they have us rave
Or disfigure ourselves, or be strangled
Like some ancient emperor's slave?

None of my dead friends were emperors
With such exorbitant tastes
And none of them were so vengeful
As to have all their friends waste
Waste quite away in sorrow
Disfigured and defaced.

I think the dead would want us
To weep for what *they* have lost.
I think that our luck in continuing
Is what would affect them most.
But time would find them generous
And less self-engrossed.

And time would find them generous
As they used to be
And what else would they want from us
But an honoured place in our memory,
A favourite room, a hallowed chair,
Privilege and celebrity?

And so the dead might cease to grieve
And we might make amends
And there might be a pact between
Dead friends and living friends.
What our dead friends would want from us
Would be such living friends.

II

Out of the East

Out of the East

Out of the South came Famine.
Out of the West came Strife.
Out of the North came a storm cone
And out of the East came a warrior wind
And it struck you like a knife.
Out of the East there shone a sun
As the blood rose on the day
And it shone on the work of the warrior wind
And it shone on the heart
And it shone on the soul
And they called the sun – Dismay.

And it's a far cry from the jungle
To the city of Phnom Penh
And many try
And many die
Before they can see their homes again
And it's a far cry from the paddy track
To the palace of the king
And many go
Before they know
It's a far cry.
It's a war cry.
Cry for the war that can do this thing.

A foreign soldier came to me
And he gave me a gun
And he predicted victory
Before the year was done.

He taught me how to kill a man.
He taught me how to try.
But he forgot to say to me
How an honest man should die.

He taught me how to kill a man
Who was my enemy
But never how to kill a man
Who'd been a friend to me.

You fought the way a hero fights –
You had no head for fear
My friend, but you are wounded now
And I'm not allowed to leave you here

Alive.

Out of the East came Anger
And it walked a dusty road
And it stopped when it came to a river bank
And it pitched a camp
And it gazed across
To where the city stood
When
Out of the West came thunder
But it came without a sound
For it came at the speed of the warrior wind
And it fell on the heart

And it fell on the soul
And it shook the battleground

And it's a far cry from the cockpit
To the foxhole in the clay
And we were a
Coordinate
In a foreign land
Far away
And it's a far cry from the paddy track
To the palace of the king
And many try
And they ask why
It's a far cry.
It's a war cry.
Cry for the war that can do this thing.

Next year the army came for me
And I was sick and thin
And they put a weapon in our hands
And they told us we would win

And they feasted us for seven days
And they slaughtered a hundred cattle
And we sang our songs of victory
And the glory of the battle

And they sent us down the dusty roads
In the stillness of the night
And when the city heard from us
It burst in a flower of light.

The tracer bullets found us out.
The guns were never wrong
And the gunship said Regret Regret
The words of your victory song.

Out of the North came an army
And it was clad in black
And out of the South came a gun crew
With a hundred shells
And a howitzer
And we walked in black along the paddy track
When
Out of the West came napalm
And it tumbled from the blue
And it spread at the speed of the warrior wind
And it clung to the heart
And it clung to the soul
As napalm is designed to do

And it's a far cry from the fireside
To the fire that finds you there
In the foxhole
By the temple gate
The fire that finds you everywhere
And it's a far cry from the paddy track
To the palace of the king
And many try
And they ask why
It's a far cry.
It's a war cry.
Cry for the war that can do this thing.

My third year in the army
I was sixteen years old
And I had learnt enough, my friend,
To believe what I was told

And I was told that we would take
The city of Phnom Penh
And they slaughtered all the cows we had
And they feasted us again

And at last we were given river mines
And we blocked the great Mekong
And now we trained our rockets on
The landing-strip at Pochentong.

The city lay within our grasp.
We only had to wait.
We only had to hold the line
By the foxhole, by the temple gate

When
Out of the West came clusterbombs
And they burst in a hundred shards
And every shard was a new bomb
And it burst again
Upon our men
As they gasped for breath in the temple yard.
Out of the West came a new bomb
And it sucked away the air
And it sucked at the heart
And it sucked at the soul
And it found a lot of children there

And it's a far cry from the temple yard
To the map of the general staff
From the grease pen to the gasping men
To the wind that blows the soul like chaff
And it's a far cry from the paddy track
To the palace of the king
And many go
Before they know
It's a far cry.
It's a war cry.
Cry for the war that has done this thing.

A foreign soldier came to me
And he gave me a gun
And the liar spoke of victory
Before the year was done.

What would I want with victory
In the city of Phnom Penh?
Punish the city! Punish the people!
What would I want but punishment?

We have brought the king home to his palace.
We shall leave him there to weep
And we'll go back along the paddy track
For we have promises to keep.

For the promise made in the foxhole,
For the oath in the temple yard,
For the friend I killed on the battlefield
I shall make that punishment hard.

Out of the South came Famine.
Out of the West came Strife.
Out of the North came a storm cone
And out of the East came a warrior wind
And it struck you like a knife.
Out of the East there shone a sun
As the blood rose on the day
And it shone on the work of the warrior wind
And it shone on the heart
And it shone on the soul
And they called the sun Dismay, my friend,
They called the sun – Dismay.

Blood and Lead

Listen to what they did.
Don't listen to what they said.
What was written in blood
Has been set up in lead.

Lead tears the heart.
Lead tears the brain.
What was written in blood
Has been set up again.

The heart is a drum.
The drum has a snare.
The snare is in the blood.
The blood is in the air.

Listen to what they did.
Listen to what's to come.
Listen to the blood.
Listen to the drum.

The Ballad of the Imam and the Shah
An Old Persian Legend

TO C.E.H.

It started with a stabbing at a well
Below the minarets of Isfahan.
The widow took her son to see them kill
The officer who'd murdered her old man.
The child looked up and saw the hangman's work –
The man who'd killed his father swinging high.
The mother said: 'My child, now be at peace.
The wolf has had the fruits of all his crime.'

From felony to felony to crime
From robbery to robbery to loss
From calumny to calumny to spite
From rivalry to rivalry to zeal

All this was many centuries ago –
The kind of thing that couldn't happen now –
When Persia was the empire of the Shah
And many were the furrows on his brow.
The peacock the symbol of his throne
And many were its jewels and its eyes
And many were the prisons in the land
And many were the torturers and spies.

From tyranny to tyranny to war
From dynasty to dynasty to hate
From villainy to villainy to death
From policy to policy to grave

The child grew up a clever sort of chap
And he became a mullah, like his dad –
Spent many years in exile and disgrace
Because he told the world the Shah was bad.
'Believe in God,' he said, 'believe in me.
Believe me when I tell you who I am.
Now chop the arm of wickedness away.
Hear what I say. I am the great Imam.'

From heresy to heresy to fire
From clerisy to clerisy to fear
From litany to litany to sword
From fallacy to fallacy to wrong

And so the Shah was forced to flee abroad.
The Imam was the ruler in his place.
He started killing everyone he could
To make up for the years of his disgrace.
And when there were no enemies at home
He sent his men to Babylon to fight.
And when he'd lost an army in that way
He knew what God was telling him was right.

From poverty to poverty to wrath
From agony to agony to doubt
From malady to malady to shame
From misery to misery to fight

He sent the little children out to war.
They went out with his portrait in their hands.
The desert and the marshes filled with blood.
The mothers heard the news in Isfahan.
Now Babylon is buried under dirt.
Persepolis is peeping through the sand.
The child who saw his father's killer killed
Has slaughtered half the children in the land.

From felony
to robbery
to calumny
to rivalry
to tyranny
to dynasty
to villainy
to policy
to heresy
to clerisy
to litany
to fallacy
to poverty
to agony
to malady
to misery —

The song is yours. Arrange it as you will.
Remember where each word fits in the line
And every combination will be true
And every permutation will be fine:

From policy to felony to fear
From litany to heresy to fire
From villainy to tyranny to war
From tyranny to dynasty to shame

From poverty to malady to grave
From malady to agony to spite
From agony to misery to hate
From misery to policy to fight!

I Saw a Child

I saw a child with silver hair.
Stick with me and I'll take you there.
    Clutch my hand.
    Don't let go.
The fields are mined and the wind blows cold.
The wind blows through his silver hair.

The Blue Vein River is broad and deep.
The branches creak and the shadows leap.
    Clutch my hand.
    Stick to the path.
The fields are mined and the moon is bright.
I saw a child who will never sleep.

Far from the wisdom of the brain
I saw a child grow old in pain.
    Clutch my hand.
    Stay with me.
The fields are mined by the enemy.
Tell me we may be friends again.

Far from the wisdom of the blood
I saw a child reach from the mud.
    Clutch my hand.
    Clutch my heart.
The fields are mined and the moon is dark.
The Blue Vein River is in full flood.

Far from the wisdom of the heart
I saw a child being torn apart.
     Is this you?
     Is this me?
The fields are mined and the night is long.
Stick with me when the shooting starts.

Tiananmen

Tiananmen
Is broad and clean
And you can't tell
Where the dead have been
And you can't tell
What happened then
And you can't speak
Of Tiananmen.

You must not speak.
You must not think.
You must not dip
Your brush in ink.
You must not say
What happened then,
What happened there
In Tiananmen.

The cruel men
Are old and deaf
Ready to kill
But short of breath
And they will die
Like other men
And they'll lie in state
In Tiananmen.

They lie in state.
They lie in style.
Another lie's
Thrown on the pile,
Thrown on the pile
By the cruel men
To cleanse the blood
From Tiananmen.

Truth is a secret.
Keep it dark.
Keep it dark
In your heart of hearts.
Keep it dark
Till you know when
Truth may return
To Tiananmen.

Tiananmen
Is broad and clean
And you can't tell
Where the dead have been
And you can't tell
When they'll come again.
They'll come again
To Tiananmen.

Hong Kong, 15 June 1989

The Ballad of the Shrieking Man

A shrieking man stood in the square
And he harangued the smart café
In which a bowlered codger sat
A-twirling of a fine moustache
A-drinking of a fine Tokay

And it was Monday and the town
Was working in a kind of peace
Excepting where the shrieking man
A-waving of his tattered limbs
Glared at the codger's trouser-crease

Saying

Coffee's mad
And tea is mad
And so are gums and teeth and lips.
The horror ships that ply the seas
The horror tongues that plough the teeth
The coat
The tie
The trouser clips
The purple sergeant with the bugger-grips
Will string you up with all their art
And laugh their socks off as you blow apart.

The codger seeming not to hear
Winked at the waiter, paid the bill
And walked the main street out of town

Beyond the school, beyond the works
Where the shrieking man pursued him still
And there the town beneath them lay
And there the desperate river ran.
The codger smiled a purple smile.
A finger sliced his waistcoat ope
And he rounded on the shrieking man

Saying

Tramps are mad
And truth is mad
And so are trees and trunks and tracks.
The horror maps have played us true.
The horror moon that slits the clouds
The gun
The goon
The burlap sacks
The purple waistcoats of the natterjacks
Have done their bit as you can see
To prise the madness from our sanity.

On Wednesday when the day was young
Two shrieking men came into town
And stopped before the smart café
In which another codger sat
Twirling his whiskers with a frown

And as they shrieked and slapped their knees
The codger's toes began to prance
Within the stitching of their caps
Which opened like a set of jaws
And forced him out to join the dance

Saying

Arms are mad
And legs are mad
And all the spaces in between.
The horror spleen that bursts its sack
The horror purple as it lunges through
The lung
The bung
The jumping-bean
The I-think-you-know-what-you-think-I-mean
Are up in arms against the state
And all the body will disintegrate.

On Saturday the town was full
As people strolled in seeming peace
Until three shrieking men appeared
And danced before the smart café
And laughed and jeered and slapped their knees

And there a hundred codgers sat.
A hundred adam's apples rose
And rubbed against their collar studs
Until the music came in thuds
And all the men were on their toes

Saying

Hearts are mad
And minds are mad
And bats are moons and moons are bats.
The horror cats that leap the tiles

The horror slates that catch the wind
The lice
The meat
The burning ghats
The children buried in the butter vats
The steeple crashing through the bedroom roof
Will be your answer if you need a proof.

The codgers poured into the square
And soon their song was on all lips
And all did dance and slap their knees
Until a horseman came in view –
The sergeant with the bugger-grips!

He drew his cutlass, held it high
And brought it down on hand and head
And ears were lopped and limbs were chopped
And still the sergeant slashed and slew
Until the codger crew lay dead

Saying

God is mad
And I am mad
And I am God and you are me.
The horror peace that boils the sight
The horror God turning out the light.
The Christ
Who killed
The medlar tree
Is planning much the same for you and me
And here's a taste of what's in store –
Come back again if you should want some more.

On Sunday as they hosed the streets
I went as usual to pray
And cooled my fingers at the stoup
And when the wafer touched my tongue
I thought about that fine Tokay

And so I crossed the empty square
And met the waiter with a wink
A-sweeping up of severed heads
A-piling up of bowler hats
And he muttered as he poured my drink

Saying

Waiting's mad
And stating's mad
And understating's mad as hell.
The undertakings we have made
The wonder breaking from the sky
The pin
The pen
The poisoned well
The purple sergeant with the nitrate smell
Have won their way and while we wait
The horror ships have passed the straits —
The vice
The vine
The strangler fig
The fault of thinking small and acting big
Have primed the bomb and pulled the pin
And we're all together when the roof falls in!

Fireflies of the Sea

Dip your hand in the water.
Watch the current shine.
See the blaze trail from your fingers,
Trail from your fingers,
Trail from mine.
There are fireflies on the island
And they cluster in one tree
And in the coral shallows
There are fireflies of the sea.

Look at the stars reflected
Now the sea is calm
And the phosphorus exploding,
Flashing like a starburst
When you stretch your arm.
When you reach down in the water
It's like reaching up to a tree,
To a tree clustered with fireflies,
Fireflies of the sea.

Dip your hand in the water.
Watch the current shine.
See the blaze trail from your fingers,
Trail from your fingers,
Trail from mine

As you reach down in the water,
As you turn away from me,
As you gaze down at the coral
And the fireflies of the sea.

Cut-Throat Christ

or the New Ballad of the Dosi Pares

Oh the Emperor sat on an ivory throne
And his wives were fat and all their jewels shone
And the Emperor said: It's plain to see
Christ was an emperor just like me.

Well the rich have a Christ and he's nobody's fool
And he pays for their kids to go to convent school
And their momma drives them home to tea.
She says: Christ is a rich bitch just like me.

But *I* say:

I say he sold his body to some foreign queer
And he sold his blood for just a case of beer
And he sold his soul to the fraternity.
Christ became a cut-throat just like me.

There's a Christ for a whore and a Christ for a punk
A Christ for a pickpocket and a drunk
There's a Christ for every sinner but one thing there aint –
There aint no Christ for any cutprice saint.

Well I was casting for fish by the North Harbour Pier
When this guy called Jesus says to me: Come here –
If you want to join the fraternity,
Lay down your nets and you can follow me.

So I left my nets and I left my line
And I followed my Jesus to the Quiapo shrine
And he told me many stories of his enemy –
It was General Ching of the EPD.

And I swore to the Black Nazarene there and then
I'd go out and kill one of the General's men
And when I brought my *beinte-nuebe* for the boss to see
That guy called Jesus he was proud of me.

Oh the Emperor sat on an ivory throne.
He had twelve brave peers and he loved each one.
We were twelve disciples and our strength was proved
But I was the disciple whom Jesus loved.

There's a Christ for a whore and a Christ for a punk
A Christ for a pickpocket and a drunk
There's a Christ for every sinner but one thing there aint –
There aint no Christ for any cutprice saint.

Well Jesus was a drinker as you might expect.
We got through plenty stainless and a few long necks
And then Jesus got mad as mad can be.
He said: One of you punks is gonna squeal on me.

Now that General Ching has put a price on my head
With disciples like you I'm as good as dead –
There's one who will betray me to the EPD.
We said: Tell me boss, tell me boss, is it me?

But there wasn't the leisure and there wasn't the time
To find out from Jesus who would do this crime
For a shot rang out and we had to flee
From General Ching and half the military.

Oh the Emperor sat on an ivory throne
And out of twelve brave peers there was just one bad one
And Christ had twelve disciples and they loved him so
But one out of twelve is just the way things go.

There's a Christ for a whore and a Christ for a punk
A Christ for a pickpocket and a drunk
There's a Christ for every sinner but one thing there aint —
There aint no Christ for any cutprice saint.

Well I ran like crazy and I ran like fuck
And for the next three days I did my best to duck
And then I made my way back to the EPD.
I said: The General said he had a job for me.

Well the General he saw me and his face grew grim.
He said: Watch it guys, don't stand too close to him —
That's our old friend Judas and he wants his fee,
But the guy called Jesus he is roaming free.

I said: What's the deal? He said: We killed him, sure,
We filled him full of what we had and then some more,
We dumped him back in Tondo for his momma to see
And now he's resurrected with a one, two, three.

I said: General Ching, if what you say is true
I'm gonna need some protection out of you.
He said: Just pay him off now and let me be —
We don't protect a mediocrity.

'Cos the Emperor sat on an ivory throne
But that was long ago and now the Emperor's gone
And this guy called Jesus he is something new:
You crucify him once and he comes back for you.

We've dumped him in the Pasig, we've thrown him in
the Bay,
We've nixed him in the cogon by the Superhighway,
We've chopped him into pieces and we've spread him
around
But three days later he is safe and he is sound.

There's a Christ for a whore and a Christ for a punk
A Christ for a pickpocket and a drunk
There's a Christ for every sinner but one thing there aint –
There aint no Christ for any cutprice saint.

Now Manila's not the place for a defenceless thing –
You either go with Jesus or with General Ching
And I'd been with both and after what I'd been
I knew my only hope was the Black Nazarene.

So I go barefoot down to Quiapo and the streets are
packed
And they're carrying the Nazarene on their backs
And just one step and it's plain to see
That Christ will crush them to eternity –

The Christ of the Aztecs, the Juggernaut God,
The Christ of the Thorn and the Christ of the Rod
And they're carrying the Christ along two lengths of
rope
'Cos the Cut-Throat Christ's a cut-throat's only hope

And there's the man who killed the Carmelites, the
Tad-tad gang,
The man who sells the Armalites in Alabang
And General Ching, the EPD, the senatorial bets,
The twelve disciples and the drum majorettes,

The Emperor Charlemagne, the rich bitch and the
    queer,
The guy called Jesus by the North Harbour Pier
And they're coming down to Quiapo and they've all
    made a vow
To wipe the sweat from the Black Nazarene's brow.

Oh the Emperor sat on an ivory throne
But in a cut-throat world a man is on his own
And what I've got is what you see –
Cut-Throat Christ, don't turn your back on me.

Gabriel

I come home to the cottage.
I climb the balcony.
It's the archangel Gabriel
Waiting there for me.

He says: Boss, boss, cut the loss,
Don't take on so.
Don't get mad with Gabriel.
Let it go.

I go into the kitchen
To fix myself a drink.
It's the archangel Gabriel
Weeping by the sink.

He says: Boss, boss, cut the loss,
Don't take on so.
Don't get mad with Gabriel.
Let it go.

I say: You've been away in Magsaysay,
You've not clocked in all week;
You're as strong as an ox,
But you're work-shy
With your head bowed low and your pleading eyes
And I'm too mad to speak.

I come home two hours later.
The archangel drops a tear.
He's sitting there in the same old chair
And he's drunk all the beer.

He says: Boss, boss, cut the loss,
Don't take on so.
Don't get mad with Gabriel.
Let it go.

I say: You've drunk yourself into outer space.
You're giving me one of those looks.
You're as wild as the moon in storm time
And I'd like to know the reason I'm
Supposed to keep you on the books.

Yes I should have known when I took you on
When you tumbled from the sky
That you're set in your ways and that's all.
You're a Gabriel and you've had a fall.
You can't change and nor can I
Gabriel
You can't change and nor can I.

The Ballad of the Birds

There's a mynah bird a-squawking
In the ipil-ipil tree.
I say: What do you want,
What do you want,
What do you want from me?
For my crops have all been planted
And the rainy season's here
But the baby in the hammock
Will not see out the year

And it goes

Crack crack
I'll be back
I'll be back like a heart attack
I'll be back when your hopes are wrecked
I'll be back when you most expect

There's a turtle dove a-weeping
In the crest of the dap-dap tree.
I say: What do you want,
What do you want,
What do you want from me?
For my son has gone to Saudi
And my daughter's in the States
But I'll have to borrow money
And I can't afford the rate

And it goes

Coo coo
Hard on you
Crack crack
I'll be back
I'll be back like a heart attack
I'll be back when your hopes are wrecked
I'll be back when you most expect

And the kingfisher goes shrieking
At the edge of the shining sea.
I say: What do you want,
What do you want,
What do you want from me?
For my wife has gone to the graveyard
To clear the weeds away
And the rains have failed and the land is dry
And there'll be some grief today

And it goes

Kraa kraa
Life is hard
Coo coo
Hard on you
Crack crack
I'll be back
I'll be back like a heart attack
I'll be back when your hopes are wrecked
I'll be back when you most expect

There are sparrows in the paddy
On the road to the cemetery.
I say: What do you want,
What do you want,
What do you want from me?
There's a grief that knocks you senseless.
There's a grief that drives you wild.
It picks you up.
It throws you down.
It grabs your hair.
It throws you in the air.
At the coffin of a child

And it goes

Peep peep
A child comes cheap
Kraa kraa
Life is hard
Coo coo
Hard on you
Crack crack
I'll be back
I'll be back like a heart attack
I'll be back when your hopes are wrecked
I'll be back when you most expect

Oh I'm nothing but a farmer
In the harvest of the year
And the rains have failed
And the land is sold
And I'm left in grief and fear

And there's a carrion crow alighting
On the crest of the banyan tree.
I say: What do you want,
What do you want,
What in the name of God do you want from me?

I Know What I'm Missing

It's a birdcall from the treeline.
I hear it every day.
It's the loveliest of the songbirds
And I'm glad it comes this way
And I stop to listen
And forget what I've to do
And I know what I'm missing –
My friend
My friend.

It's a fluttering in the palm fronds
With a flash of black and gold.
It's the whistling of the oriole
And its beauty turns me cold
And I stop to listen
And forget what I've to do
And I know what I'm missing –
My friend
My friend.

Do you wonder if I'll remember?
Do you wonder where I'll be?
I'll be home again next winter
And I hope you'll write to me.
When the branches glisten
And the frost is on the avenue
I'll know what I'm missing –

My friend
My friend
I'm missing you.

Bruisers and Dreamers

The leading lights of Bulacan
The bruisers and the dreamers
Are politicians to a man.
Their names go on the streamers.

But if their man's an also-ran
The dreamers and the bruisers
Mingle beneath the ceiling-fan
With schemers and Yakuzas.

To work and thrive as best they can
The bruisers and the dreamers
Take forged assignments in Japan
By cruisers and by steamers.

But when they meet the mamasan
The toughest of the bruisers
Back out and hide upon the can.
The dreamers make the excusers.

It's hard to live in Bulacan
For bruiser as for dreamer
But it's harder when the mamasan
Is Yukio Mishima!

God bless them all in Bulacan.
God bless them all in Lima.
God bless us all, whate'er our tan —
Each bruiser and each dreamer.

Here Come the Drum Majorettes!

There's a girl with a fist full of fingers.
There's a man with a fist full of fivers.
There's a thrill in a step as it lingers.
There's a chance for a pair of salivas –

For the

Same hat
Same shoes
Same giddy widow on a sunshine cruise
Same deck
Same time
Same disappointment in a gin-and-lime

It's the same chalk on the blackboard!
It's the same cheese on the sideboard!
It's the same cat on the boardwalk!
It's the same broad on the catwalk!

There's a Gleb on a steppe in a dacha.
There's a Glob on a dig on the slack side.
There'a a Glubb in the sand (he's a pasha).
There's a glib gammaglob in your backside

Saying

Gleb meet Glubb.
Glubb meet Glob.
God that's glum, that glib Glob dig.

'Dig that bog!'
'Frag that frog.'
'Stap that chap, he snuck that cig.'

It's the same ice on the race-track!
It's the same track through the pack-ice!
It's the same brick in the ice-pack!
It's the same trick with an ice-pick!

There's a thing you can pull with your eyeballs.
There's a tin you can pour for a bullshot.
There's a can you can shoot for a bullseye.
There's a man you can score who's an eyesore.

I'm an
Eyesore.
You're the thing itself.
You've a
Price or
You'd be on the shelf.
I'm a loner
In a lonesome town –
Barcelona –
It can get you down.

It's the same scare with a crowbar!
It's the same crow on the barstool!
It's the same stool for the scarecrow!
It's the same bar!

Ho!

Ha!

Like a spark from the stack of a liner
Like a twig in the hands of a dowser
With the force of the fist of a miner
(With the grace and the speed of a trouser)

In a

Blue moon
In a blue lagoon
She's got blue blue bloomers in a blue monsoon.

Wearing blue boots
And a blue zoot suit
He's a cruising bruiser with a shooter and a cute little
Twin blade
Sin trade
In a
Blue brown
New Town.

It's the same hand on the windpipe!
It's the same sand in the windsock!
It's the same brand on the handbag!
It's the same gland in the handjob!

The room is black.
The knuckles crack.
The blind masseuse walks up your back.
The saxophone
Is on its own
Pouring out the *Côtes du Rhône*.

When you're down to your last pair of piastres.
When you're down on your luck down in Przemyśl,

When your life is a chain of disasters
And your death you believe would be sameish,

When the goat has gone off with the gander
Or the goose with the grebe or the grouper
Then – a drum majorette – you can stand her:
She's a brick – she's a gas – she's a trouper

Saying

Jane meet John.
John meet Jane.
Take those jimjams off again
Jezebel.
Just as well.
Join the jive with Jules and June.
Geoffrey, Jesus, Jason, Jim,
Jenny, Jilly, Golly Gee –
If it's the same for you and him
It's the same for you and me:

It's the same grin on the loanshark!
It's the same goon in the sharkskin!
It's the same shark in the skin-game!
It's the same game
Same same

It's the same old rope for to skip with!
It's the same Old Nick for to sup with
     With a long spoon
     To the wrong tune

And it's hard for a heart to put up with!

III

Maski Paps

The Orange Dove of Fiji

TO R. & B. O'H.

On the slopes of Taveuni
The Barking Pigeons woof
But when I saw the Orange Dove
I nearly hit the roof

And would have surely had there been
A roof around to hit
But the roofs of Taveuni
Are down on the lower bit

While up there in the forest
The Silktails have survived
Where they 'forage in the substage'
And you feel you have *arrived*

As an amateur ornithologist
In the midst of a silktail flock
Until you hear behind you
A 'penetrating tock'

And you find six feet above your head
What you were looking for –
The Orange Dove of Fiji,
No less, no more.

The female of the Orange Dove
Is actually green.

The really orange *male* Orange Dove
Is the one you've seen.

It must have been dipped in Dayglo
Held by its bright green head.
The colour is preposterous.
You want to drop down dead.

It turns around upon its perch
Displaying all the bits
That are mentioned in Dick Watling's book
And the description fits.

Then it says: 'Tock — okay, is that
Enough to convince you yet?
Because that, my friend, is all tock tock
That you are going to get.'

Oh the Many-Coloured Fruit Dove
Is pretty enough to boot
And I'm afraid the purple swamphen
Looks queerer than a coot

Like a flagrant English Bishop
Let loose among his flock
With brand-new orange gaiters
(And that's just the swamphen cock)

But the Orange Dove is something
Spectacular to see
So I hope they don't fell another single
Taveuni tree.

The Journey

Every girl has four vaginas.
Boys are one vagina minus.

In the vagina of the hand
Every festival is planned.

In the vagina of the mouth
All the compasses point South.

In the vagina of the dark
There's no decent place to park.

But in the vagina of the moon
A boy may swim too far, too soon,

Beyond the reef, beyond the bay,
Beyond where all the breakers play

And, like the snorkeller, turn again
To see his childhood flecked with rain.

For every girl and every boy
Seeks a journey to enjoy

And four plus four, and three plus three,
In God's numerology

Comes to nought, and three plus four
Comes to a bundle at the door

And they unwrap the wretch to see
Is it four? or is it three?

For every girl has four vaginas
But boys are one vagina minus.

On a Recent Indiscretion by a Certain Fulbright Fellow in Upper Egypt

He fell among the fellahin.
He felt a fellow feeling.
They went in an alfalfa field
Where they began unpeeling.

The muezzin he caught sight of them
From the high minaret
And what he saw made him as mad
As a holy man can get.

He foamed and fumed and frothed at them
Then pelted them with quince.
That Fulbright Fellow has not faced
His fellow Fellows since.

A fast felucca ferried him
Past the Nile's fair fronded fringes
But when he reached his consulate
His mind was off its hinges.

'Farewell to the falafel farm,
Farewell the *ful medames*,
Farewell the fez, the Fatimids,
Farouk in my pajamas,

'Far from these fair fringe benefits
My feeble prospects beckon

And I shall fray my future away
In frigging Llanfairfechan.'

The fellah in this episode
Who hailed from Wadi Halfa
Has found that Fulbright Fellowship
Where it lay in the alfalfa

And fiendishly invested it
In French securities
To furnish his foul flock with funds
For forseeable dynasties.

And the moral of this episode
May be set forth forthrightly:
Don't go fellating fellahin!
You're a Fulbright Fellow! It's unsightly!

Maski Papaano

Kung mayron, mayron.
Kung wala, wala.
Fish, kamatis,
Meat, patatas,
Maski paps, pala.

IV
The Manila Manifesto

Nagdadaláng takot, hiya't alang-alang
nag-aalapaap yaring gunam-gunam
mapuról na noo at dilang mabagal
iwaksí ang takot at kapanganiban.

Sa actualmenteng aking pagkatayo
indecibleng tuwa'y kinamtang ng puso
saan mangagaling at saan hahango
sabing conveniente sa tanáng pinuno.

Pupunuan ko na yaring sasabihin
anhin ang maraming kuntil-butil
di raw mahahapay kahoy na puputlin
kung yamba nang yamba't di tuluyang tagin.

What you need for poetry is a body and a voice. It
doesn't have to be a great body or a great voice. But
it ought ideally to be *your* body, and it ought to be *your*
voice.

The parent helps the child discover what may be done
with its lips and its limbs. This is the first poetry.

A sort of night then falls – a melancholy mercy – after
which the initiation is mysteriously forgotten. This is
the primal erasure.

The remainder of our lives is spent in recapturing that
initial sense of discovery. This is the second poetry.

But the wisdom of the age has forbidden us the use of
our lips and our limbs. This wisdom is the enemy of
poetry.

You call yourself a poet?
Don't you see, you're incomplete
With your double-nelson plaster cast
And your disenfranchised feet?

In Madame Vendler's Chamber of Horrors I saw seven
American poets, strung up by their swaddling-bands
   and crying: More Pap! More Pap!

A foreign body
Dug up in Manila
In a state of advanced decay
Turned out to be that
Of Theophilus Pratt
Who resumes supervision today
In L.A.

I saw seven beautiful women, the dreaded Manananggal
of Atimonan, who, as I approached, arose and flapped
away and I perceived they had left behind the lower
part of their bodies. 'Mga Manananggal, Mga
Manananggal,' I cried after them, 'saan ang punta.'
They hung momently in the flowering crest of the
Dapdap tree. 'Pupunta kami sa IOWA, pare ko,'
laughed one, and they clattered off over the Pacific.

Prayer

'Lord, give me back my body
And give me back my voice.'
'Son, I would give your body back
But alas I have no choice.

'For you have pawned your arms and legs,
Your fingers and your toes
And you sold your voice to the bottle-boy
For twenty-one pesos.'

'Oh Lord, redeem my pawn-ticket
And find that bottle-boy too.'
'Your ticket, son, has passed its date
And your body is glue

'And the bottle-boy has pushed his cart
Back home to his Tondo slum
And the Sigue-Sigue Sputnik gang
They laughed to see him come

'And they snatched away your voice from him
For he sang so tunefully
And they slit the throat of the bottle-boy
And they threw him in the sea

'And they passed your voice from hand to hand
And your song was in their mouth
And they went to war with the Tad-tad gang

And the Ativan gang
In Alabang
By the Superhighway South.

'For seven days and seven nights
Your voice rose o'er the fray
And you would tremble had you heard
The things I heard you say.'

I saw Emily Dickinson in a vision and asked if it was merely by coincidence that so much of her poetry could be sung to the tune of 'The Yellow Rose of Texas'. She said: 'In poetry there is no coincidence. I had feet once. I had knees. I would not have you think I had no knees.'

Pain like the Flemish!
Give weight to the blemish!

Down with a cautious perfection!
Down with a bloodless circumspection!

So you despise my fecklessness?
I pity your lack of recklessness.

This is the new fearlessness.
That is the old earlessness.

This is the new recklessness.
That is the old what-the-hecklessness.

Voici la Nouvelle Insouciance.
Voilà . . . hein?

Die Neue Rücksichtlosigkeit —
I would pronounce it if I might
Von Ewigkeit bis Ewigkeit —
Die Neue Rücksichtlosigkeit.

An arrow was shot from Teheran. A novelist lifted a shield. A thousand arrows were shot from Boston. A thousand poets died.

We call on America to stop killing, torturing and imprisoning its poets.

Sa Kusina

Ako'y Pilipino
Pili at pipino
Sili, luya
At sibuyas —
Ako'y Pilipino.

Blank terror doth stalk
The poets of New York.

The Exchange

I met the Muse of Censorship
And she had packed her bags
And all the folk of Moscow
Were hanging out the flags.

I asked her what her prospects were
And whither her thoughts did range.
She said: 'I am off to Dublin town
On a cultural exchange.

'And folk there be in Cambridge
Who like the way I think
And there be folk in Nottingham
Whom I shall drown in ink

'And when we reach America
The majorettes will sing:
Here comes the Muse of Censorship –
This is a very good thing.'

I went to the Finland Station
To wave the Muse goodbye
And on another platform
A crowd I did espy.

I saw the Muse of Freedom
Alighting from the train.
Far from that crowd I wept aloud
For to see that Muse again.

The Approval

You tell me that your poems
Have been approved in France.
Well, that settles that!
Or aren't you ashamed, perchance

To cite this recognition
On the grounds that it's French.
What language do you feel in?
You make me blench.

This is no time for people who say: this, this, and only this. We say: this, and *this*, and *that* too.

An Amazing Dialogue

'But this poem is not like that poem!'
'No, you are right, it's not.'

The Poetry of Pure Fact

One prawn
with an ablated eye
can spawn
as many as one million fry.

We despise terrorist normative critics.

We despise the deformed, uncandid class-consciousness of our domestic criticism. On our map, there are no compass points. North, for instance, does not mean good.

We say to France: AUT TACE AUT LOQUERE MELIORA SILENTIO – either shut up or say something worth saying.

A Poem against Barn Owls

Some people think that barn owls
are an endangered species
but they are found all round the world
as are their faeces.

The Gene-Pool

Get out of the gene-pool, Gene,
And take your tambourine.
You write the way you speak.
You're not one of our clique.
You say the things you mean.
Out of the gene-pool, Gene.

Get out of the gene-pool, Gene,
And go behind that screen.
You don't respect our style.
You sometimes crack a smile.
Your insouciance is obscene.
Out of the gene-pool, Gene.

You don't belong to our age.
You don't 'write for the page'.
You put us in a rage.
You are unclean!
Get out! Get out!
Out of the gene-pool, Gene.

An Indistinct Inscription Near Kom Ombo

(Meroitic Cursive)

I was born to a kiss and a smile.
I was born to the hopes of a prince.
I dipped my pen in the Nile
And it hasn't functioned since.

The Answer

'Stop! Stop! Stop!
Stop in your tracks.
Because you are not with us
You are holding everyone back.'

'Friend, you and your friends go your way
And I'll go mine.
I've enough water to survive
But far too little wine.'

(Crocodilopolis Papyrus no. 10743)

Notes

Many of the poems in this volume were originally published in *Manila Envelope*, a privately printed volume which came with 'The Manila Manifesto' and a poster. The songs in the section called 'Out of the East' were put together under that name as a pocket musical and were first performed on 21 November 1990 by the National Theatre at the Petit Odéon in Paris. The music, which is published by Faber & Faber, is by Dominic Muldowney. The original production had two singers, Robyn Archer and Richard Walsh. Dominic Muldowney played piano, David Roach alto saxophone and flute. The director was Di Trevis and the designer Alison Chitty.

In the ballad 'Cut-Throat Christ', the *dosi pares* are the Twelve Peers of Charlemagne, whose legend was retailed in the old Tagalog ballads. Today the term *dosi pares* is often used to indicate a criminal gang, both in Manila and in the provinces. A *beinte-nuebe* is a kind of butterfly knife, so called after its 29-centimetre blade. 'Stainless' is a kind of gin, a 'long neck' refers to any 75 centilitre bottle of spirits. The statue of the Black Nazarene is to be found in the Quiapo church in the market area of down-town Manila. Of seventeenth-century origin and Aztec workmanship, it is the object of a widespread cult particularly among members of the underworld. Dick Watling's book is called *Birds of Fiji, Tonga and Samoa*.